GUESS AND LEARN
Magic Words
Please, Sorry, Thank You, and More!

by **Pauline Y. Atilite**
Illustrated by **Afzal Khan**

Remember to always say *please* while making a request. This indicates politeness and respect.

Remember to always say *thank you* when someone helps you, gives you something, or offers advice. It shows your appreciation.

Remember to always ask for *help* when you are facing a difficult time or situation because no human knows, or can do, everything.

Remember to always say *excuse me* when trying to get someone's attention because it is a polite way to interrupt someone.

Remember to always say *sorry* when your mistake has caused pain or discomfort to another person. Apologies are a sign of strength.

Remember to always spread the love around you. Even simple acts of kindness, like telling others *I love you*, can help someone feel better.

MAGIC WORDS IN SIGN LANGUAGE

Have someone help you point out these magic words.
Point to the magic words you use the most.

THANK YOU   PLEASE   HELP

EXCUSE ME   SORRY   I LOVE YOU

MAGIC WORDS IN MY LIFE

- Can you name a time when you might say *please*?
- When would you say *sorry*?
- When was the last time you said *thank you*?
- What things do you need *help* with most?
- To whom do you say *I love you* to express your affection?
- Can you name a time that you might say *excuse me*?
- What magic word do you struggle with, and why?